I HAVE ADHD, WHY NOT?

IT'S MY BRILLIANCE AND NOT MY DISORDER

Redefining The Beauty of An Unstructured Mind

SHEILA MAE BALAGA

Published by House of Tap to Shift
www.taptoshift.com
Copyright © 2025 by Sheila Mae Balaga
All rights reserved.
ISBN: 979-8-9937437-0-7

Table Of Contents

PREFACE – WHY I WROTE THIS BOOK

A letter to the misunderstood minds. The truth about how society defines disorder, and how self-acceptance became the quiet revolution.

(Includes the story and evolution of how ADHD was once misunderstood and how it continues to awaken through time.)

PART 1 – THE SYSTEM THAT GOT IT WRONG

Chapter 1 The Classroom That Couldn't See Me
> When obedience was praised more than curiosity, and imagination was mistaken for defiance.

Chapter 2 The Rules That Broke My Spirit
> How discipline without understanding turned light into silence.

Chapter 3 Pretending To Be Normal
> The mask of fitting in and the moment it began to crack.

PART II — HOW MY BRAIN ACTUALLY WORKS

Chapter 4 Curiosity in Motion
> The beauty of a non-linear mind and the wisdom in wandering.

Chapter 5 Flow Over Focus
> How attention moves through emotion, intuition, and energy.

Chapter 6 Energy, Emotion, and the Sacred Cycle
> Understanding the waves of burnout, brilliance, and rebirth.

PART 111 – FLOW, CREATIVITY AND REBELLION

Chapter 7 When Structure Becomes Suppression
What happens when systems crush the soul's natural rhythm.

Chapter 8 The Gift They Called Disorder
Redefining the meaning of "too much" and why it's everything the world needs.

Chapter 9 The World That Can't Keep Up
How we're reshaping the definition of intelligence, creativity, and success.

PART IV — GRATITUDE FOR THE GIFT

Chapter 10 Brilliance in Motion
Learning to receive ease, flow with inspiration, and live unapologetically aligned.

Chapter 11 For Every Mind That Ever Felt Wrong
A final reflection, the reclamation of difference as divine design.

Afterword — A Letter to the Reader
Understanding the waves of burnout, brilliance, and rebirth.

Before You Read

Before you begin, take a deep breath. Let your shoulders soften. Let the world outside this page slow down for a moment and breathe it all out.

I want you to read this book not with your mind, but with your frequency. with the part of you that feels beyond words. Allow the pages to speak directly to your consciousness. Let them move through you rather than be analyzed by you.

This book wasn't written to make perfect sense. It was written to make you feel and experience it. The sentences you'll find here were not built from rules or formulas, they were written through flow. I didn't try to make every line sound right. I let the words breathe. I gave them space to find their own rhythm, just like I had to find mine.

There is no right or wrong way to receive what's here. Some lines might land like truth, others might drift past like a breeze and that's okay. Trust what resonates. Let go of what doesn't. Every page carries its own current. My only wish is that you allow yourself to flow with it, without needing to control it.

For those who seek structure, perfection, or predictability; may this book be your permission to rest from all of that. My words are unstructured on purpose. They mirror how my brain works; nonlinear, bouncy, curious, and spirited.

The Earth needs both order and flow, form and movement. So do we.
This book is my flow written into form. Let it speak to yours. Let it soften something inside you and above all, let it remind you that even in your unstructured ways, you are whole

Preface:
Why I Wrote This Book

Part I — The Calling to Write

I didn't sit down to write this book because I wanted to teach something. I wrote it because I needed to understand myself.

For a long time, I carried this quiet ache that sense of being different in a world that only loved what it could define. I didn't have the words for it back then. All I knew was that my mind didn't move the way everyone else's did. I was fast when life wanted slow, and slow when the world demanded speed.

When I finally heard the word ADHD, it didn't feel like a discovery. It felt like being named after years of invisibility, only it wasn't the kind of name that set me free. It sounded clinical, sharp-edged, sterile like something to be managed instead of understood.

I spent years trying to live the way the world expected. I learned how to fake focus, how to blend in, how to suppress the pulse of curiosity that lived inside me. I became good at pretending to be ordinary. Even then, inside, something kept stirring, that familiar hum of restlessness that whispered, "There's more to you than what they see."

I wrote this book because I finally decided to listen to that voice.
Writing became the only space where I could exist without rules. On the page, I could think, feel, and express without being corrected or contained. I could write in my own rhythm, in a way my mind could actually absorb. The page didn't punish me for wandering or changing my mind; it welcomed it. It let me follow the thread of a thought until it found something meaningful, something that felt true to me. In words, my untamed parts and fluidity made sense.

This book is that space; a reflection of how my ADHD mind works when it's free. Short paragraphs, open spaces, easy to read, fast to finish and thoughts that breathe. It doesn't follow the usual structure, because neither do I.

There's something sacred about being in your own flow. Every sentence became a mirror. Each paragraph is a breath of recognition. The more I write, the more I realized I was shifting to who I truly am.

I began remembering all the versions of me that were misunderstood; the girl who talked too much, who lost her focus mid-thought, who lived in an in-between world while her eyes were open, dreaming in images instead of plans, and who even now struggles to define herself by a single career title. I started to see her not as a problem, but as part of my essence, something written into my DNA.

This book is for her and for everyone who's ever felt unseen by the systems that claim to help them because the truth is, most of us were taught to value silence over curiosity, compliance over creativity, control over connection. We were told that the mind must move in straight lines, and anything else was a flaw to fix. Except that's not how the human spirit works. It was never meant to fit inside a single rhythm.

So I wrote this as a gentle rebellion. The kind that doesn't need to shout to be heard. A rebellion made of acceptance. When I look back, I realize this book didn't start with a diagnosis. It started the moment I decided to stop apologizing for how I exist. It started the day I realized I could love a mind that moves like water; unpredictable, fluid and always searching for the hidden threads beneath everything.

This isn't a book about ADHD as a condition. It's about ADHD as an experience, it's a lens, a rhythm, a way of seeing the world. It's about what happens when the mind refuses to obey the rules of order and instead follows the rules of being.

I wrote this because I wanted to give shape to something that has been misunderstood for generations. What if the point was never to cure it? What if the point was to understand it?

If you're holding this book, maybe you've felt it too, that quiet friction between who you are and what the world expects. Maybe you've spent years trying to make sense of a brain that doesn't move in straight lines. Maybe you've blamed yourself for being too much or not enough. I know that feeling. I know it very well.

And I also know what it feels like to finally stop running from it. I didn't write this as someone who has everything figured out. I wrote it as someone still learning how to be in rhythm with her own genetic. Every chapter is a memory, a realization, a piece of healing and together, they tell the story of what it means to live in a mind that was never meant to be tamed.

So if you've ever felt like you don't belong, like your thoughts move too fast, or your feelings run too deep, I hope this book reminds you that maybe you were never meant to fit. Maybe you were meant to see differently. And maybe, just maybe, that difference is your brilliance.

Part II — The History of ADHD

Before I could write about ADHD as a gift, I had to understand why it was ever called a disorder. So, I began to look back. I traced its history through time, through names and systems that tried to define it. What I found wasn't just a story about medicine or psychology, it was a story about control, misunderstanding, and how society has always feared what it can't categorize.

The Beginning: When Difference Was Called Defect

In the early 1900s, a British doctor named **George Still** wrote about children who couldn't follow directions, sit still, or restrain their impulses. He said they had a **"Defect Of Moral Control."** Those words stayed with me — **Moral Control.**

What he was really saying was that good children follow rules and those who don't must be defective. It was the beginning of something bigger than just a diagnosis. It was the start of how society began to confuse obedience with intelligence.

Back then, the world was rebuilding itself through structure; factories, schools, churches, governments, all designed around one thing: **Order.** People were expected to move in rhythm with the machine. The mind, too, had to obey. So, what happened to the ones who couldn't? They became the misunderstood; the dreamers, the restless, the ones with too much energy and too many questions.

From "Moral" to "Medical"

As decades passed, science replaced morality, but not the judgment. By the 1930s, they called it **"Minimal Brain Dysfunction."** The language shifted from defect to dysfunction but the meaning stayed the same, that something inside you is wrong and yet, no one could prove what was wrong.

There were no brain scan, blood test, and no single explanation. It was just observation, repetition, and a world desperate to make sense of behavior that didn't match its structure.

Then came the 1950s, when medicine found a way to calm the storm. Stimulants were discovered; pills that could quiet the movement, the talking, the energy. For the first time, society could control what it didn't understand. Children who couldn't sit still could now be managed and once again, the difference was contained.

The Invention of the Word "ADHD"

In 1980, the label changed again. Now, it had a new name —
ADD, or **Attention Deficit Disorder**. It sounded modern, scientific
and clinical.

But still, it carried the same undertone, that we were missing
something. It's a deficit, lack and an absence of what was
considered normal.

By 1987, it evolved once more into **ADHD** — **Attention-
Deficit/Hyperactivity Disorder.** That word — **DISORDER** —
would follow us for decades. Yet when I read the descriptions, I
didn't see a disorder. I saw sensitivity, curiosity and intensity.

All the things that made life vibrant for me, but unbearable for
those who needed predictability. It made me realize that the
problem wasn't the mind. The problem was **the measurement.**

What the System Couldn't See

Every era defined ADHD according to its own priorities. In the 1900s, when society valued obedience, disobedience became wrong. By the 1950s, productivity was the measure of worth, so distraction became wrong. And by the 2000s, focus was prized above all else, turning wandering minds into something to fix. Yet what if all those 'wrongs' were actually signs of human evolution?

ADHD, I began to see, wasn't a malfunction. It was a mirror, reflecting what happens when the human spirit doesn't fit the systems built to contain and control it. We've never been sick. We've just been too vibrant for a world that doesn't know how to hold that vitality.

The Shift Begins

Somewhere around the late 1990s and early 2000s, things began to change. The internet gave voice to those who had never been heard. People began sharing their stories not as patients, but as people and for the first time, we started to see the pattern.

So many of us had lived the same life; misunderstood in classrooms, mislabeled in workplaces, misjudged in relationships. We weren't lazy. We were wired differently. That's when the term **neurodiversity** entered the conversation, the idea that the human brain naturally comes in different shapes, rhythms, and speeds.

And that maybe, just maybe, the goal was never to make everyone the same, but to learn how to thrive in our own unique design. It was the first time in history that ADHD was described not as a defect, but as a variation and that changed everything.

Beyond Science

Even as I read through studies, data, and theories, something deeper in me knew that science could describe how we think, but not why. There's something sacred about how our minds work.

We see things before others do. We feel the undercurrents. We process emotion and possibility at the same time. Maybe that's not a disorder at all. Maybe that's evolution in motion because when you look closely, ADHD attention is tied to internal rhythm. It's attune to movement, to emotion, to the rhythm of nature itself. Our minds don't drift aimlessly; it follow energetic shifts and intuitive timing. We're tuned to a frequency that listens to flow rather than structure.

It's not about hyperactivity. It's about expression, there's an energy inside us that wants to move, create, and respond to what feels alive. The world calls it restlessness, but it's really responsiveness. It's not that we can't focus. It's that we can't fake interest and in a world built on repetition, that kind of authenticity can look like rebellion.

The Real History

So, when I look back now, I don't see a medical timeline. I see a spiritual one. A history of humanity trying to define what it doesn't yet understand. From moral defect to minimal brain dysfunction to attention disorder, every label shows more about society than it does about us. Each stage tells the story of a world that still hasn't learned how to honor difference but it's learning slowly and we're the proof.

We've survived centuries of misunderstanding and somehow, we still create, imagine and feel deeply enough to write books like this one. The world once called it a disorder but I see it now as genetics; one that's teaching us to remember what it means to be human again.

Part III — The Evolution of Understanding

I read through the history of ADHD and realized something; the diagnosis wasn't born from understanding; it was born from confusion and that confusion was never about the mind itself. It was about humanity's fear of what it can't organize.

For so long, we've lived in systems that glorify discipline; schools built for conditioning, workplaces built for control, and lives built around obedience and order. The world defines worth by productivity and titles, yet many ADHD minds struggle to answer questions like "Who are you?" or "What do you do?" because our interests shift, evolve, and expand. We live in constant becoming so our souls still exploring all our potential paths.

People with ADD and ADHD aren't unfocused, we're multi-focused. Our attention isn't absent; it's everywhere at once. We might start one task, then another, then chase a thought that turns into an idea, and suddenly we've followed ten threads at once. From the outside, that looks like distraction but from the inside, it feels like drifting without an anchor, like being lost in a sea of possibilities. Everything feels alive, and we want to touch all of it.

In that kind of world, any mind that doesn't move in straight lines gets labeled as unhinged. But what if being unhinged isn't madness at all? What if it's brilliance that just hasn't found its rhythm yet? Because we are navigators of our inner worlds. We don't get lost because we're wrong. We get lost because we see too much.

The Turning Point

There was a time when I believed everything I was told about ADHD, that it was a flaw, a dysfunction, a challenge to overcome but the more I lived in this body, the more I felt the truth stretch underneath those words because if this was a flaw, why did it feel so fired up when I followed it? If this was dysfunction, why did it lead me to such creativity, insight, and intuition?

The more I questioned, the more I began to see that ADHD isn't a disorder of attention, it's a different relationship with attention. We don't lose focus; we flow with it. We don't lack discipline; we move where energy feels real for us. We don't fail to prioritize; we simply can't fake what we don't feel and that realization changed everything. My brain wasn't disobedient at all, it was just pure honest.

Science Begins to Listen

When I began learning how the brain actually works, the story started to make sense. Science discovered that people with ADHD don't have less focus, we have more pathways of attention, more sensitivity to stimulation, more active networks lighting up all at once.

Our minds aren't quiet because they were never meant to be. They're designed to explore, connect, and create links that others can't see. That's why our thoughts jump from one thing to another because everything is connected.

We feel life in full spectrum. We sense patterns, possibilities, and potential before they form into words. That's not a deficit. It's intuition but science still tried to name it clinically, to contain it in explanations and categories. It's like trying to trap lightning in a jar. You can study the light but you'll never understand what makes it move.

The Rise of Neurodiversity

When the idea of neurodiversity started to spread, something clicked inside me. It was the first time I saw the word diversity beside the word "Neuro". As if finally, the mind was being honored as part of the natural design of difference. Neurodiversity said that there isn't one correct way to think, focus, feel, or function.

And I thought, yes, that's it. We were never meant to be identical because we were meant to be in tune. We're not supposed to operate like machines; we're supposed to move like music, and each of us has a different instrument, playing a different rhythm. The world had called ADHD unpredictable, but maybe it's not unpredictability at all. Maybe it's rhythm that doesn't fit the world's beat.

The Mirror of the Modern World

As I grew older, I started to notice something deeper, that ADHD doesn't just reflect the individual mind; it mirrors the collective one. The world itself has become overstimulated; screens, social media, noise, schedules, endless to-do lists. We are living in a planet-wide attention crisis. Everything demands focus, yet nothing holds meaning for long.

Maybe the reason ADHD feels so common now isn't because more people are "disordered." Maybe it's because we've been trained and conditioned to become dysregulated in our consciousness, to the point where we've forgotten what real even feels like.

Those of us with ADHD, the ones who feel too much, think too fast, and move too freely are mirrors showing the imbalance. We can't sit still in systems that have lost their soul, we can't focus on what feels false and we can't pretend to be fine when the energy is wrong, because we're not the problem. We're awake to a system that fractures the mind and confuses the self that lives within it.

From Surviving to Understanding

When I began to accept this truth, my relationship with myself softened. I stopped seeing ADHD as a battle to win and started seeing it as a language to learn and like all languages, it has its rhythm; sometimes fast, sometimes scattered, sometimes still. It's a living language of consciousness, because ADHD speaks in energy. It flows within our system.

That's why we have a hard time following structure because we follow spark. Our motivation is fueled by emotional and energetic connection and not on external pressure or duty. When we feel energized, we can give it everything. When it feels dull, forced, or meaningless, our brain simply won't respond. It's like our body is asking, "Give me something real, something raw, something that moves me." because it's one of our languages.

We don't think before we feel, we feel as we think. Our emotions are interwoven with cognition. That's why we love deeply, react quickly, and process the world through our intuition and empathy. We don't speak in cold logic. Stillness can feel like suffocation to an ADHD mind. Our thoughts move, so we need to move too. We speak in emotion, sensation, and meaning; it's our energetic rhythm.

The ADHD body mirrors our ADHD mind; both are always searching for flow. When someone tries to teach or lead us without emotional connection, the message doesn't land because the emotional current is the message. Movement, sound, light, and texture all become part of how we communicate with the world.

We express through pacing, doodling, creating, tapping, dreaming. It's our way of saying, "I'm processing." Our ADHD mind doesn't see one path, it sees many. That's why we connect dots others miss, innovate under pressure, and imagine outcomes no one else considers because our mind speaks in potential. So when systems demand linear progress, we naturally clash because our mind doesn't move step by step. It moves in leaps, spirals, and sparks.

So in essence, the language of ADHD is energy, emotion, movement, possibility, and authenticity. It's the language of life itself; unfiltered, primal, and visceral. When the world stops trying to discipline that language and starts listening to it, we'll stop calling it a disorder.

Collective Understanding

Today, the conversation around ADHD is changing. We're beginning to see it not as a limitation, but as evolution, a new kind of intelligence rising through the cracks of outdated systems.

The classroom of the past wanted memorization. The world of the future needs imagination. The office of the past wanted obedience. The future needs innovation and who better to lead that shift than the ones who have always seen things differently?

Collectively, we are learning to understand it more deeply with empathy, curiosity, and acceptance. As the world learns to adapt to our way of being, evolution itself accelerates. Society begins to breathe differently.

We stop forcing everyone into one rhythm and start honoring the diversity of tempo; the fast, the deep, the nonlinear, the intuitive. Innovation thrives when difference is not silenced but understood.

When the world makes space for the ADHD mind, creativity expands. Our Workplaces become more supportive, progressive and forward-thinking. Education becomes more conscious, engaging and expansive. Communication becomes more transparent, genuine and honest.

Our way of seeing; fast, feeling, and fluid pushes evolution forward. We connect what's been separated, we find patterns in chaos, and we bring movement where systems have grown rigid. When the collective learns to move with us instead of against us, it learns to flow, to feel, and to create again. That's how society benefits, we become more intuitive, creative, and emotionally intelligent together.

Innovation accelerates because ADHD minds see connections others overlook. We spark new ideas, new technologies, and new ways of thinking. Our nonlinear minds help humanity imagine beyond logic by building bridges between worlds that once seemed unrelated.

Systems become more human. When workplaces and schools adapt to neurodiverse rhythms, we move away from control and toward collaboration. Structure becomes flexible. Learning becomes experiential. Work becomes purpose-driven. We stop rewarding compliance and start rewarding curiosity.

Our emotional awareness deepens because ADHD sensitivity teaches the world empathy. We feel what others suppress. We mirror truth. even when it's uncomfortable and as society learns to hold that level of sensitivity, and relationships whether it's personal, professional, and collective become more authentic and connected.

Furthermore, our creativity leads progress. We bring color to what's gray and rhythm to what's routine. Our impulsivity becomes innovation when met with understanding. Society stops merely surviving, we start creating.

Our collective balance returns because our world has lived too long in the masculine polarity of discipline, order, and repetition. ADHD energy reintroduces the feminine polarity; intuition, emotion, and flow.

When both coexist, evolution becomes sustainable. When the collective makes room for ADHD beings, society learns how to move with life again and not against it.

We remind the world that efficiency without soul is emptiness, and that speed without meaning is emptiness in motion. By learning and accepting us, the collective remembers what it once forgot, that being fully ourselves was never about control. It was always about mutual recognition, shared identity and joint experience.

By recognizing us, we grow as one, because authenticity enhances everyone, and we restores our sense of belonging because we're not outsiders to fix, we're part of the same tribe and the same collective consciousness we are all breathing.

What It Means to Understand

To understand ADHD isn't to explain it. It's to witness it and to see a child drawing on the margins of their notebook and recognize that art as thinking. It's to see someone lost in thought and realize they're not absent, they're deep in another world. It's to see someone restless and know that their energy is looking for purpose and not permission.

Understanding ADHD is learning to love motion, to honor minds that move differently, to trust that creativity can't be contained in routine. It's realizing that brilliance isn't about control, it's about in harmony and maybe that's what we were always trying to teach the world.

When I think about the history of ADHD now, I don't see the evolution of medicine. I see the evolution of awareness. Each era peeled back another layer from stigma to diagnosis, silence to recognition, shame to acceptance and now we're entering the next chapter, where difference isn't just tolerated but celebrated because the truth is simple is that we don't need to be cured. We need to be seen and once we are fully, freely, without judgment that's where the brilliance unfolds.

Part IV — My Personal Revelation

Understanding something in theory is one thing, but feeling it, living it, breathing it, embodying it, that's where healing begins. For years, I collected information about ADHD. I watched videos, read studies, listened to podcasts. I wanted to understand my brain the way the world did with logic, structure, and proof but the more I learned, the less peace I felt. The facts gave me clinical, sterile, and logical understanding; I understood the labels, the criteria, and the medical framing, but they didn't give me relief. It took me a long time to realize that the mind can't be healed by analysis alone. Healing happens the moment you stop fighting yourself, and that was my revelation. I didn't need to fix my mind. I needed to love it.

The Quiet Shift

It didn't happen overnight. It wasn't a dramatic awakening. It was more like a quiet homecoming, a small realizations that began to build a bridge between who I was and who I had been pretending to be. I noticed how hard I tried to appear "put together." How I masked my scattered edges in professionalism. How I'd apologize when I forgot something, even when my heart was full of care.

I had this constant fear of disappointing people, of being "too much," or "too inconsistent," or "too emotional." But one day, I asked myself a simple question: What if I stopped apologizing for being who I am in my own way? That question changed everything.

It felt radical to let myself exist without explanation and to finally honor my pace, my rhythm, my bursts of energy, and my quiet withdrawals. I began noticing the moments when my energy flowed correctly of how easily I could create, connect, learn, and move. I noticed how drained I felt when I forced myself into things that didn't feel natural. That was my body's wisdom showing me that I wasn't disobeying, I was discerning.

When the Mask Fell Off

There's a moment every person with ADHD eventually faces; the day you stop performing and finally meet yourself. For me, that moment came when I was tired, not just physically, but emotionally. Tired of pretending to be a version of myself that was acceptable to others and holding my breath in systems that suffocated my authenticity. So I stopped. I let the mask fall and when it did, something miraculous happened, I didn't collapse. I expanded because the truth was. the mask had been heavier than the mind ever was, without it, I started to notice beauty again in my sensitivity, in my spontaneity and in my emotional depth.

The very things I had once labeled as problems became portals. My forgetfulness turned into creativity. My impulsivity turned into intuition. My restlessness turned into movement toward growth. It was like learning a language I had been speaking all along but never understood until now.

Reclaiming My Rhythm

I started to create routines that made sense for me, not for society. I gave myself permission to work with my energy, not against it. If I needed movement, I moved. If I needed silence, I honored it. I began to see patterns in my own rhythm, bursts of deep creation followed by stillness, waves of focus followed by flow.

I stopped calling it inconsistency. I started calling it cycle. I stopped calling it distraction. I started calling it divine curiosity because that's what ADHD really is; A mind that doesn't obey the clock. The call and that realization brought me so much peace and for the first time, I wasn't chasing balance. I was living in harmony within myself.

Seeing Myself Clearly

When I look back now, I see a younger version of myself; the girl sitting at a desk, crying in the library, trying to make sense of her state of mind. Tapping her pen in frustration, drowning in disappointments, and feeling worthless about herself.

I wish I could step into a time machine from the future, from this version of me, and whisper to her, 'You are not scatterbrained or unreliable, my love. You are vibrant and full of ideas. Your energy is too big for the box you were placed in, because you were never meant to be tamed. Your mind was meant to be free."

Because every late assignment, every scolding, every drift of thought; they were all signs of a mind that needed to breathe. I wish someone had told me then that I wasn't behind. I was ahead, just in a way the world didn't recognize yet.

That little girl who once cried herself to sleep because she couldn't understand her own mind. The thing she once thought was a wound that needs to be cured is now writing to enlighten and empower the world with the very pain she once thought was a burden, but instead, turned out to be her gift and her power. I wish she knew that, and now I wish you know this.

Living the Revelation

Healing didn't mean I stopped being forgetful or restless. It meant I stopped judging myself for it. Now, when I lose focus, I remind myself that maybe it's not time for that task. When I hyperfocus, I trust the magic that flows through me. When I feel overwhelmed, I rest not because I'm weak but because I'm wise enough to know when my system needs space.

I don't try to control my brain anymore. I collaborate with it. I've learned that peace doesn't come from structure; it comes from self-understanding and understanding happens when you finally meet yourself where you are and not where you think you should be.

The Deeper Meaning

Maybe ADHD was never meant to be my struggle. Maybe it was my initiation, my path back to authenticity. Every misunderstanding, frustration and label, they were all invitations to remember who I am beneath the noise.

The world called it a disorder, but my soul calls it a divine blueprint. A way of seeing that is raw, vivid, intuitive, and honest and maybe that's the real gift of it all, is to live in a mind that feels everything and still chooses love. It's what I came to realize that alignment doesn't mean becoming normal. Alignment means becoming yourself fully.

Part V — A Note To Ponder

If you're holding this book right now, maybe a part of you already knows that you've never been the problem. Maybe you've spent years trying to explain yourself to people who could never meet you where you are. Maybe you've been told that you're inconsistent, unreliable and messy. When all you ever were was being lit from within in a way the world wasn't ready for. Maybe you've carried shame for a mind that wanders, or a heart that feels too much, or energy that doesn't follow the clock. If that sounds like you, this is for you.

I want you to know that your difference is not a flaw. It's the rhythm of your genetics. You were never meant to sit still in a world that moves without meaning. You were never meant to obey systems that silence intuition. You were never meant to shrink your brilliance just to appear stable and sane. The world has confused stillness with success for far too long but some of us were born to move, sense, shift, and connect patterns that no one else can see.

We're not here to keep up; we're here to wake things up. There's a reason your curiosity won't stop asking why. There's a reason your energy comes in waves, of why you light up when something feels right and fade when it doesn't.

There's a reason you can feel a room's truth before anyone speaks. That's not dysfunction. That's sensitivity as intelligence. Your mind isn't failing you; it's searching. Your attention isn't structured ; it's selective and intentional. It refuses to attach to what's false and that is one of the most powerful instincts you could ever carry.

You might have been called difficult. You might have been told to calm down, to be realistic, and to focus but what they really meant was, 'Be smaller so we can understand you.' And yet here you are, still trying, still feeling, and still reaching for meaning in a world that often confuses numbness for discipline.

You've survived misunderstanding after misunderstanding, and you're still choosing to know yourself. That's courage and brilliance.

I wrote this book for you, not to fix or simplify you, but to stand beside you in truth. To remind you that being human was never meant to look one way. That maybe your so-called free-moving rhythm is just creativity untamed. That maybe your sensitivity is how you stay connected to what's real.

If no one has ever said it to you before, let me be the first: Your brain is not malfunctioning. Your heart is not too much. Your energy is not a curse. They are all parts of your intelligence.

So, take a deep breath.... Unclench the years of trying to be someone else. Let this book be a space where you don't have to explain yourself anymore.

Here, you can just exist, exactly as you are. Your attention doesn't need correction and your difference is sacred because underneath every label, every struggle, and every misunderstanding, there's a constant truth: You were always meant to be this way and maybe, just maybe, you came here to remind the rest of the world what unfiltered existence, spaciousness, liberation and sovereignty really looks like.

Part I:
The System That Got It Wrong

Chapter 1: The Classroom That Couldn't See Me

Back when I was in school, I didn't know what ADHD even meant. It wasn't a word anyone used in the Philippines, it was invisible, non-existent. We grew up in a culture where order was everything. You followed rules, respected authority, and behaved politely. That was the expectation. So when I didn't fit that mold, I assumed something was wrong with me.

I was always the student who got in trouble, the one who came late, talked too much, or forgot instructions halfway through. Teachers said I wasn't listening, but I was. I just wasn't listening to them. My mind had already wandered into other worlds, drawn to questions and ideas far beyond the lesson on the board. It wasn't disobedience at first; it was curiosity without boundaries but in a world built on compliance, curiosity can look like defiance.

I remember how I used to stare at the window during class, my thoughts spinning faster than the clock on the wall. I'd imagine entire stories from the smallest things: a bird passing by, a flicker of light on the chalkboard, a whisper between classmates. Everything caught my attention except what I was supposed to pay attention to.

One day in class, I got completely lost in my own world. I was so focused on putting white baby powder all over my face and if you grew up in the Philippines in the '90s, you'd understand, Johnson's Baby Powder was our version of foundation back then. I was blending it on my face, totally unaware that class had already started.

Then suddenly, my teacher called my name. 'Sheila!' I jolted up like lightning, completely forgetting that my entire face was still covered in white powder. The whole class froze for a second, staring at me like they'd just seen a ghost. And then it happened... everyone burst out laughing.

So there I was, standing with my ghost-white face, laughing along even though I had absolutely no idea what was funny yet. But the moment it hit me, the moment I realized I was the joke, the laugh got stuck in my throat and turned into tears. And the funniest part? My teacher made me stand there like a classroom ghost, powder and all, while she continued her lesson. And honestly... I just wanted to disappear like a real ghost.

I remember feeling humiliated, terrified, and so mad at myself for not listening. That was one of the first moments I started believing I was "a problem." I didn't know then that I wasn't being careless, I was just being me.

Oh the routine, Oh God. I hated the routine; waking up early, memorizing facts, pretending to care about subjects that didn't made sense to me, it just drained me. The repetition and monotony hurt my soul. Some mornings, I'd make up excuses just to stay home.

Many times, I put garlic on my armpit. In many Filipino households, especially in earlier generations, people believed that rubbing garlic (bawang) on underarms could make someone's body feel warm, even warm enough to "fake" a fever.

The idea comes from traditional beliefs that garlic has heating properties. It increases blood flow and can slightly irritate the skin, creating a warm sensation or even mild redness. So when my mother touched my skin, she'd believe I wasn't well and let me stay home.

That way, I could miss school; escape the conditioning of the same looping experiences on a daily basis and be alone with my imagination. Television, stories, books and music fed my spirit in a way the classroom never could.

Looking back, I see it clearly now, school was never built to feed my brilliance. It was structured to tame it.

The Illusion of Discipline

In the Philippines, being a "good student" meant being quiet, obedient, and disciplined. Those were the markers of respect. Teachers didn't mean harm, they were following what society believed was right.

But when I look back now, I realize that discipline, in that form, wasn't about learning. It was about control. We were taught to follow strict rules before we were taught to think. To memorize before we were encouraged to imagine.

To behave before we were allowed to feel. And so, from a young age, I learned to associate success with compliance. I thought that if I could just follow the order better, I'd finally fit in. But no matter how hard I tried, my mind refused to be managed. It wanted to dance when everyone else marched. It wanted to ask why when everyone else said 'Yes, Ma'am.' It wanted to create, connect, and question but that kind of mind didn't belong in a classroom designed to reward obedience so I followed.

The Misunderstanding

I didn't realize it back then, but every time I got in trouble, it wasn't because I was being difficult, it was because my nature was misunderstood. I was punished for movement, corrected for curiosity and scolded for excitement. And over time, those experiences began to plant a quiet belief inside me, that being in my flow was somehow wrong.

I started to shrink. I started to silence the parts of me that were too loud, too eager, too vibrant, too excited, and too curious. I became the student who pretended to listen, who forced herself to stay still, who hid her restlessness behind smiles. But no matter how well I performed, something inside me knew, I wasn't learning, I was trying to survive.

The Mind That Refused to Conform

My mind needed space to move, to feel, to wonder but instead, it was told to sit still and follow what was asked of me. So it rebelled. Every day felt like being trapped in a rhythm that didn't match my internal song. My attention didn't disappear; it just refused to attach itself to anything meaningless. I wasn't unmotivated, disengaged, or slow. I was just starving for stimulation, for connection, for something real, something that made sense to my heart.

It's strange how the things that get you in trouble as a child often become your greatest strengths later in life. The same imagination that made me "distracted" became my creative gift. The same sensitivity that made me "too emotional" became my intuition. The same curiosity that made me "hard to teach" became the force that fuels everything I write. I didn't know it then, but my so-called flaws were never meant to be erased, they were meant to be heard and understood.

The Moment of Awareness

Over time, I learned how to survive within the system. I learned how to pretend, how to manage my attention just enough to get by. But inside, something deeper was happening, that old soul within me whispering to save me from being conditioned, 'Don't lose yourself to who you are not.' It was the part of my spirit that refused to be bruised by conformity.

For years, I thought I was a defect in society, a problem to fix, a student who couldn't follow the traditional path. I didn't know then that I was simply different, and difference, when misunderstood, always looks like disorder.

Chapter 2: The Rules That Broke My Spirit

Growing up, I thought being a good person meant being obedient and polite. That was what I saw, what I was taught, and what I learned to embody. "Follow the rules." "Be respectful." "Don't question adults." "Do what's right, even when it doesn't make sense."

These weren't just lessons. They were laws, unspoken spiritual codes that shaped how we lived and for a long time, I believed them wholeheartedly but there's a quiet danger in growing up inside a culture that values obedience more than authenticity. You learn how to follow everything and everyone except yourself.

The Shape of Obedience

In the Philippines, children are raised with respect as the foundation of identity. We're taught to use honorifics like po and opo, to greet elders, to lower our tone, to behave properly in front of others. It's beautiful in its intention, to teach humility and harmony.

But the shadow side of that beauty is silence. Respect slowly becomes fear. Obedience turns into erasure. You learn that speaking up is rude. That disagreeing is opposition. That questioning is disrespect. So I learned to hold everything in, the questions, the confusion, the emotions that didn't fit the rules and when you do that for long enough, your body becomes your prison.

I remember how my chest would tighten every time I wanted to say something but couldn't. How my throat would burn from words that had nowhere to go. I thought I was learning discipline but really, I was learning disconnection.

The Culture of Comparison

Growing up, obedience wasn't the only rule, there was another one sewn into my culture itself, a quieter one beneath it: Blend in, follow the script everyone else followed. Do well in school, graduate, pick a practical college degree, preferably something more respected like nursing or any career with a clear ladder so you could make money, support your family, and earn your place in society. That was the path, 'keep up, rise up, don't fall behind.'

No one ever wrote it down, but it lived in everything on how we were graded, praised, compared, and corrected. And truly, it came from love, from wanting stability, pride, and the chance to survive, succeed, and make the people we care about proud. For many, that path works beautifully. Structure fits them and surely routine grounds them. But for someone wired like me, that same path felt like a cage. Trying to bend myself into that shape felt like losing the very essence of who I was.

Conformity was the currency of belonging. So I learned early how to measure myself through others. Their approval became my validation. Their expectations became my purpose and every time I couldn't keep up, when I forgot instructions, missed deadlines, or lost focus, I felt it as a personal failure and not a symptom of misalignment because that's what conditioning does, it makes you doubt your own truth in favor of everyone else's comfort.

When the Mind Splits from the Soul

As I got older, the rules multiplied. Be polite. Be productive. Be patient. Be organized. Be perfect. No one said it out loud, but the message was clear: The world rewards the ones who can pretend best. So I tried.

I became who they needed me to be. I silenced my impulses. I masked my energy. I shrank every time my intensity made others uncomfortable and on the outside, it worked. I looked functional, grounded, responsible and mature. But inside, I was dissolving because to obey everything outside of you, you have to betray something inside of you and I didn't realize how deep that betrayal went until I couldn't recognize myself anymore.

The Emotional Consequence

There's a kind of exhaustion that doesn't come from doing too much, but from being too little of yourself for too long. That's the exhaustion I lived in for years. I was tired, not from effort, but from suppression. Tired of smiling when I wanted to cry. Tired of saying yes when I meant no. Tired of making myself smaller just to fit into the expectations of people who didn't even know my soul. I thought this was what being good meant, sacrificing your truth for peace. But peace built on silence isn't peace. It's survival mechanism.

The Awakening Beneath the Rules

It took me years to see the pattern: Every rule I followed was built on fear; fear of being rejected, fear of being misunderstood, fear of being seen too clearly and that fear didn't come from me. It came from generations before me.

From parents who were taught the same thing, systems that punished nonconformity and a collective belief that order equals safety. But order without authenticity is a quiet kind of death. It kills the parts of you that are meant to grow wild and untamed and for a long time, I mistook that death for maturity. I thought discipline meant control, silence meant peace and perfection meant love. But none of it was love. It was fear dressed in obedience.

Rebellion in Disguise

What I didn't understand back then was that my ADHD, my restlessness, sensitivity, and constant questioning was never the problem. It was my soul's rebellion. It was my spirit saying, 'This isn't who you are.' Every time I got distracted, it was my intuition pulling me away from what didn't resonate. Every time I talked too much, it was my creativity looking for air. Every time I forgot the rules, it was because they were never meant for me. What the world saw as disobedience was actually alignment trying to break through conditioning. I wasn't defying authority, I was defending my authenticity.

What Those Rules Taught Me

It's strange, but I'm grateful for those rules now because they showed me the cost of disconnection. They taught me how heavy it is to live for approval. They taught me that peace built on perfection is never real peace. Most of all, they taught me what freedom actually feels like, it's not the absence of responsibility, but the presence of self. The moment I stopped obeying everything that went against my spirit, I finally heard my own rhythm again. And that rhythm; unpredictable, sensitive, and wild is the sound of my truth.

Chapter 3: Pretending to Be Normal

There's a certain kind of exhaustion that doesn't show. It hides behind smiles, achievements, and polite conversations. It lives quietly in the background of people who seem like they have it all together, people who learned early on that being normal is safer than being real. That's the exhaustion I carried for most of my life. After years of following rules, I became an expert at pretending. I learned how to blend in, how to mirror, how to make my inner storm look calm and on the surface, it worked. People thought I was responsible, mature, grounded but inside, I was constantly at war with myself.

The Art of Masking

When you grow up being misunderstood, you start to build masks to survive. You learn how to smile when you're overstimulated, how to laugh when you're anxious, how to say "I'm fine" even when your mind is running in ten directions at once.

Masking becomes a way of life. I didn't even realize I was doing it, I thought that was what "being adult" meant is to suppress my emotion, perform stability and to edit yourself until you fit what the room needs you to be.

But deep down, I knew. I knew the version of me people loved wasn't the full truth. It was the filtered one, the one I made digestible for others because somewhere along the way, I had learned that authenticity made people uncomfortable. That my energy, my intensity, my unpredictability, the things that made me me, were too much. So, I hid them.

The Weight of Perfection

I became addicted to performance, to proving my worth and overcompensating for every area where I felt different. If I couldn't be the quiet, focused student, then I could be the creative one. If I couldn't be consistent then I could at least be passionate and If I couldn't be perfect then I could at least look like I was trying harder than anyone else. It was exhausting, not physically but emotionally.

Every success felt like a cover-up for the fear that one day, people would see the real me and leave because that's what masking does, it doesn't protect you; it isolates you. It creates this distance between who you are and who you've become and the longer you live that way, the harder it gets to remember which one is real.

The Loneliness of Pretending

There's nothing lonelier than being surrounded by people who love your mask but not your truth. I was praised for my reliability, admired for my work ethic, appreciated for my calmness and yet, I felt invisible because how can someone love you if you're never really there? The more I tried to be what everyone needed, the further I drifted from myself.

I became an echo; a reflection of other people's comfort zones and the more they approved of me, the emptier I felt. Sometimes I'd look at myself in the mirror and think, Who am I when I'm not trying to be good and sane? It's a haunting question, one that most people with ADHD eventually ask because we spend so much of our lives trying to prove we're "enough" that we forget what it feels like to simply be.

The Fear of Being Found Out

There's a strange fear that comes with pretending, the fear of being seen, not seen in the sense of being noticed, but seen in the sense of being known because deep down, I was terrified that if people saw how scattered I felt inside, they'd stop loving me. That if I admitted how hard it was to stay organized, to stay focused, to stay emotionally regulated, they'd see me as weak.

So, I over-functioned, over-delivered, over-apologized. I said yes when I wanted to say no. I stayed calm when I wanted to scream. I worked through burnout just to prove I could keep up and every time I succeeded, it reinforced the illusion, that I was capable, collected, in control. No one saw the meltdown behind closed doors, the anxiety that built up after a simple mistake and the nights I stayed awake replaying every conversation, worrying if I had said too much or not enough.

The Quiet Breakdown

It didn't happen all at once. There wasn't one dramatic moment when everything fell apart. It was more like slow erosion, small cracks forming over time until the structure couldn't hold. The pretending became heavier, the mask stopped fitting and the pace became impossible to maintain.

One day, I couldn't fake it anymore. I forgot something important at work and broke down in tears, it's not because of the mistake, but because I had no energy left to hide. It was in that breakdown that I realized something had to change. I couldn't keep performing normalcy nor keep betraying myself for approval and keep apologizing for existing differently. That breakdown wasn't my failure, it was my return.

Remembering the Real Me

When I finally stopped pretending, I didn't feel powerful. I felt lost. Because I had spent so many years being someone else that I didn't know how to just be me. So, I started small. I gave myself permission to forget things without guilt. I let myself speak freely without overthinking how it sounded. I began to listen to my body instead of my calendar and in that softness, I found something I hadn't felt in years — **peace**. It's not the kind of peace that comes from control, but the kind that comes from authenticity. The kind that says, you don't have to earn your place here.

The Truth About Normal

Looking back now, I realize that "normal" is just another word for predictable and predictability might make people feel safe, but it doesn't make life meaningful. I don't want to be predictable. I want to be full of life.

Normal never inspired me; it never moved me or reflected who I am. The truth is, I was never meant to be normal. I was designed to be real, to live from pure knowing, to follow the sparks that others overlook.

My nature doesn't chase approval; it observes, learns, and leads by being. I was born to question what's accepted, to see differently, to embody my individuality as truth. It's that quiet knowing that I was here to live authentically and that is my normal.

The Freedom of Being Seen

There's nothing more liberating than being fully seen, not for the polished version, but for the raw one. The one that forgets, feels, dreams, and moves at its own pace. When I stopped pretending, I realized the people who truly loved me never needed me to be perfect. They just needed me to be honest and maybe that's what healing really is, not becoming someone new, but finally letting the truth be visible because pretending might protect you for a while, but authenticity will save you forever.

The Freedom of Being Seen

Part II:
How My Brain Actually Works

Chapter 4: Curiosity in Motion

For most of my life, people described me as distracted and unchained. They said I couldn't focus, I didn't finish what I started, My attention was scattered, floating from one idea to the next like a butterfly that could never land but that's not what it felt like on the inside. Inside, it felt expansive and electric. It felt like my mind was built to move, not in a straight line, but in spirals.

My curiosity has never been calm. It moves like water, flowing toward whatever feels exciting and when something catches my attention, it's not because I choose it. It's because it chooses me. That's what people don't understand about minds like mine. We don't chase distraction. We chase vibrancy.

The Nature of Motion

When I was younger, teachers said I needed to "stay on one thing."
But my mind didn't work that way. It wanted to connect everything.
If we were learning about history, I'd start wondering about time. If
we studied science, I'd think about emotion. If we talked about math,
I'd see patterns in people's behavior.

My thoughts didn't stay within subjects; they built bridges between
them. To others, it looked like I was off-topic, but to me, it all made
sense. That's how my brain works, it moves to understand. It doesn't
sit still and memorize; it feels its way through meaning. I've realized
that ADHD isn't an attention disorder at all; it's an attention with its
own intelligence that is attuned, adaptive, and drawn to whatever
carries real substance.

The Spark and the Flame

People with ADHD often talk about "hyper-focus" that deep tunnel where time disappears and everything else fades away. I know that place well. When I'm in it, I feel infinite. Ideas unfold like music. Every thought links perfectly to the next, and for a while, the noise of the world disappears but the spark that ignites that focus isn't control, it's connection to the infinite. I can't force it. I can only follow it.

When something resonates with my heart, my mind locks in like it's found its home. But when something feels empty or meaningless, no amount of effort can make me stay, not because I'm stubborn but because it's my truth detection. My energy naturally gravitates toward authenticity. It refuses to give attention to what isn't aligned. Once I understood that, I stopped calling myself inconsistent. I started calling myself attuned.

Curiosity as Compass

For me, curiosity isn't a personality trait, it's my survival instinct.
It's how I navigate the world, find meaning, and stay connected to life when everything feels overwhelming. When my curiosity is active, I'm unstoppable; I create, I learn, I connect. But when it fades, I collapse. My body feels heavy, my thoughts scatter, and my motivation disappears. I enter that familiar melancholic phase.

This rhythm is the creative pulse of my genetics moving through me.
It used to scare me. I thought it meant I was lazy and unmotivated.
But now I understand, curiosity is how my soul speaks. It's the sacred space between breaths of inspiration, the stillness before the next creation, where my new knowing quietly gestates.

When it quiets, it isn't a flaw; it's a signal that I've lost touch with what's real. So I've learned to follow it, to let curiosity lead instead of control. Even when my mind jumps around, I trust it's still moving toward creation because curiosity has never led me wrong; it just leads me differently.

Feeling Before Thinking

One of the most misunderstood parts of ADHD is how we process information. People assume we're impulsive or inconsistent, but the truth is, **we feel** first. Before logic, words, decisions , **we feel.**

Our minds take in the energy of things long before we analyze them. That's why environments affect us so deeply. Why we can sense tension in a room, or why someone's tone matters more than their words. Our attention doesn't respond to command; it responds to resonance. We don't focus because we "should." We focus because we care and that kind of focus can't be forced. It can only be invited.

The Dance of Distraction

Distraction, for me, isn't disruption, it's communication. When I lose focus, it's not because I'm weak-willed. It's because something in me is bored, uninspired, or emotionally disconnected. My distraction is my body's way of saying, 'This isn't for us right now.' It's easy to see that as failure, but I've learned to see it as guidance because when I honor that movement, when I pause, step back, breathe, or shift directions, my creativity returns stronger than before. It's not that I can't focus. It's that I'm not meant to waste energy forcing focus on what doesn't align. My mind was never designed for discipline through pressure. It was designed for expansion through purpose.

Creativity in Motion

When my energy is aligned, creation flows through me like a current. Ideas arrive in clusters; full scenes, solutions, and insights all at once. It's not linear, it's moving. I can write hundred of pages in one sitting, then need silence for days. I can clean my house at midnight because a thought sparked movement. I can forget to eat when I'm inspired, and forget everything else when I'm not.

I used to see that as instability. Now I see it as rhythm. It's a cycle of expansion and rest; a creative pulse that knows when to bloom and when to breathe. The more I trust that rhythm, the more balanced my life becomes. It's not in the way society defines balance through scheduled, predictable, symmetrical but in the way nature does: through flow.

The Wisdom of Movement

When I finally stopped fighting the way my mind works, I started to hear its wisdom. I realized that my movement is direction. When my mind drifts, it's leading me toward what matters.

When I feel restless, it's asking me to grow. When I lose focus, it's reminding me that not everything deserves my energy. That's how ADHD feels from the inside, it's not like a storm to control, but like wind to navigate. It's responsive and intuitive and maybe that's what curiosity truly is, it's not a desire to know everything, but a devotion to stay connected to what's real.

Chapter 5: Flow Over Focus

For most of my life, I believed that focus was the goal that if I could just concentrate harder, plan better, and discipline myself enough, I'd finally feel successful or at least normal but no matter how hard I tried, my mind always seemed to wander. I'd start something with enthusiasm, then drift away. I'd get inspired, then lose interest immediately. I'd try to force attention, but the harder I tried, the more my energy scattered. I used to think that was failure. Now I see it was guidance because my attention was never meant to be forced. It was meant to flow naturally.

The Myth of Focus

The world loves the idea of focus; Tidy, controlled, and linear. It fits neatly into schedules, systems, and metrics. But focus, as society defines it, was built for machines, it's not for human beings.

Focus says, "Pick one thing. Stick with it. Ignore everything else."
Flow says, "Follow what feels alive. Move with it. Let it change you."

For years, I tried to master focus; planners, lists, time blocks, deadlines but none of it worked for long because the truth is, my energy doesn't obey the clock, it obeys meaning and meaning can't be scheduled. When I started to trust flow instead of fighting for focus, my whole life shifted. I realized that my mind wasn't chaotic, it was just creative. It didn't want control. It wanted connection to nature.

Flow Has Its Own Logic

When I'm in flow, everything aligns. I can think, feel, and create all at once. My energy moves effortlessly, without resistance. It's not discipline that makes it happen, it's attunement. People often ask, "How do you get yourself to focus?" But the truth is, I don't. I just follow the current that's already moving through me. Flow has its own intelligence. It knows when to pull me toward and finish something and when to release me from it. It knows when to rest and when to run. Focus demands control. Flow invites trust and trust, that's the real key to living with ADHD.

When Energy Meets Meaning

The ADHD brain doesn't respond to obligation, it responds to inner truth. If something matters, our energy multiplies. If it doesn't, it vanishes. That's not a lack of willpower, that's alignment. We are designed to pour our full attention into what feels alive. When we care, we can do the work of ten people. When we don't, even simple tasks feel impossible. It's not inconsistency. It's integrity.

Our attention refuses to lie. It won't pretend to engage with something meaningless, no matter how hard we push and maybe that's not something to fix, maybe it's something sacred because what if the ADHD mind isn't distracted, but honest? What if our inability to fake interest is actually our greatest spiritual compass?

The Resistance to Flow

Still, flow isn't always easy, it's not because it's wrong, but because the world resists it. We live in a society that rewards control. schedules, deadlines and predictability. The system isn't built for sensitivity; it's built for efficiency. So when you're someone who moves by feeling, you're told you're unreliable. When your inspiration comes in waves, you're told you lack discipline. When you rest, you're told you're lazy but maybe the problem isn't the rhythm.

Maybe the problem is the world's obsession with constant productivity because flow doesn't mean instability. It means harmony, a state where energy and intention meet naturally. When I learned to stop resisting my natural flow, life began to open again. Work became expression and rest became my renewal. Focus became effortless because it wasn't forced.

The Science of Flow (In Simpler Words)

If I put it simply: When we're in flow, our brains light up differently. Instead of fighting to focus, our attention merges with what we're doing. Time dissolves, our awareness expands and our creativity takes over. ADHD minds are wired for this. We're not designed for dull repetition, we're designed for immersion. That's why we thrive in movement, music, art, conversation, creation. We're not running away from focus; we're chasing the frequency of vibrancy. The moment we stop trying to focus like everyone else, flow finds us and once it does, everything clicks into place like remembering a language you were born speaking but forgot how to use.

Learning to Trust Flow

At first, I didn't trust it. I thought if I didn't control my mind, it would drift too far but every time I surrendered to flow, it brought me exactly where I needed to go. Flow always knows. It led me to create when I thought I had nothing left. It led me to rest when I thought I was falling behind and it led me to truth when I tried to stay safe.

Focus says, "Stay still." Flow says, "Stay honest." And honesty, that's where regulation lives.

Structure as a Container, Not a Cage

People often think flow means being unstructured, but that's not true. Flow needs structure, just not the kind that suffocates. It needs space to breathe, boundaries that guide rather than confine. I've learned to build containers for my energy; gentle ones, flexible ones so that my flow has direction but not pressure.

Simple things help me by setting intentions and not strict goals, organizing by feeling, not by time and using rhythm instead of routine. When I treat structure as support, not control, my flow feels safe enough to expand and it always does.

Focus as a Byproduct of Alignment

The moment I stopped chasing focus and started listening to flow, focus found me on its own. It's funny, what I used to force now happens naturally. When I'm aligned, attention comes easily. When I'm disconnected, no amount of willpower can create it. Focus is not the goal. Alignment is, because once you're in flow, everything you do whether it's work, rest, or creation becomes effortless, it's not easy, but it's natural.

What Flow Has Taught Me

Flow taught me that attention is sacred. It's not something to control, it's something to honor. Where my attention goes, my energy follows. Where my energy goes, my life grows. So I don't force myself to focus anymore. I ask myself instead, "Where is life asking for my presence today?" That's my version of discipline now is about presence, listening and flowing.

Maybe focus is a gift for those who walk in straight lines. But flow, flow is the language of those who dance through life and I think I was never meant to walk. I was meant to dance to its rhythm.

Chapter 6: Energy, Emotion, and the Sacred Cycle

My energy has never been constant. It moves in waves, sometimes electric and unstoppable, sometimes soft and withdrawn. For years, I tried to fight those changes. When I was high-energy, I'd create endlessly; work, clean, write, talk, dream, move. And when I was low, I'd disappear; quiet, disconnected, apathetic, withdrawn and still. I thought something was wrong with me. Everyone else seemed to move in straight lines; steady, predictable, consistent but I never could. No matter how many systems I tried, how many planners or routines I forced myself into, my energy refused to obey. It took me years to realize that my energy is cyclical and cycles aren't flaws. They're the universe breathing through us.

The Rhythm of Aliveness

The world loves constancy, same energy, mood, output, every day.
But nature doesn't move that way. The ocean has tides. The moon
has phases. The earth has seasons. Everything alive moves in rhythm.
So why did I expect my energy to stay the same? My highs aren't
better than my lows, they're both part of the same pulse. The surge
creates expression. The stillness creates integration. When I fight my
lows, I lose their wisdom. When I rush my rest, I steal from my
renewal and when I ignore my emotions, I silence the very compass
that guides my flow. My ADHD doesn't just live in my mind, it lives
in my body and my body has always known the rhythm before my
logic could name it.

The Energy Curve

There are days when I wake up and feel unstoppable like my ideas are rushing through me faster than I can write them down. That's when creation feels divine. But then there are days when I can't do anything.It's not because I'm lazy, but because my energy has shifted inward. It's time to digest, reflect, or simply be still.

The old me used to panic during those moments. I'd guilt myself for not doing enough, for not 'keeping up.' But now I see it differently, it's me regenerating. Just as the inhale feeds the exhale, my productivity feeds my stillness, and vice versa. I've stopped trying to force linear motion. I let myself ebb and flow, because every pause holds purpose.

The Emotional Body

For someone like me, emotions are never small. They arrive like weather; sudden, full-bodied, all-encompassing and for the longest time, I was told that was too much. "Calm down." "You're overreacting." "Stop being so sensitive." But I've learned that sensitivity isn't weakness, it's wisdom.

My emotions don't just pass through me; they inform me. They're how I sense alignment. If something drains me, it's not right for me. If something excites me, it's my body saying yes. ADHD isn't just about attention, it's about energy flow. And energy always follows emotion. That's why I've learned to honor what I feel, even when it's inconvenient because the moment I suppress emotion, my flow shuts down but when I feel it fully, honestly, without judgment, my clarity returns.

The Sacred Pause

There's a moment after every creative surge where emptiness arrives. The mind quiets, the spark dims, the body asks to rest. I used to fear that silence. I'd think, "What if I lose my drive forever?" But now I understand the pause isn't the end. It's integration. It's where inspiration becomes embodiment. It's where understanding settles into wisdom. My body is cyclical. It's wise enough to know when to move and when to melt and the more I honor that rhythm, the more sustainable my energy becomes because when I rest, I'm not stopping. I'm deepening.

Energy as Communication

I've come to see my energy as language. When exhaustion shows up, I see it as a signal, not a setback. Restlessness doesn't feel like chaos anymore; it feels like guidance pulling me toward something new. And when inspiration floods my system, I no longer mistake it for instability, I recognize it as ignition, the spark that tells me I'm aligned.

My energy speaks through sensation, not words. It tells me where I'm aligned and where I'm leaking power. If I'm drained after a conversation, that's information. If I'm lit up after creating, that's confirmation. If I'm calm after releasing control, that's integration. My body has always known the truth long before my mind accepted it. It never lied to me. I just didn't know how to listen.

.

The Cycles Within

Living with ADHD feels like moving through all four seasons at once. **Spring** brings the rush of ideas, blooming faster than I can catch them. **Summer** is the heat of creation, bright, alive, unstoppable. **Autumn** arrives with its slowing, its reflection, its gentle release. And then there is **Winter** the quiet, the stillness, the sacred pause that prepares me for everything that comes next.

Most people only value the summer of life; the visible, productive, active energy but I've learned that my winter is just as sacred. So when winter arrives, I hibernate. It's where I gather my strength, clear my mind, and remember who I am.

Every low holds a new beginning waiting beneath it. Every rest is preparing me for another rise. So, I stopped asking, "Why can't I stay consistent?" And started asking, "What season am I in right now?"

The Balance of Acceptance

True balance isn't about staying the same. It's about staying aware.
Some days, my energy will move like fire; passionate, fast, loud.
Other days, it will move like water; quiet, slow, deep and neither one
is wrong. When I honor that duality, my life feels lighter. When I fight
it, everything becomes heavy. Balance isn't control. It's cooperation
with the cycles that already exist. My energy doesn't need to be fixed,
it needs to be respected.

The Sacred Cycle of Being

I've stopped calling it inconsistency. It's rhythm, pulse and its divine motion. Everything about me; my attention, emotion, energy moves in cycles and when I finally stopped fighting that truth, I started living in peace. The same energy that once felt unpredictable now feels sacred because it's creation. I no longer ask my energy to be constant. I ask it to be true.

Maybe that's what ADHD really is, it's not a disorder of attention, but a different relationship with rhythm. We move when inner knowing calls. We rest when truth returns. We feel deeply because life speaks to us in sensation and once we stop trying to fit into the straight lines of the world, we begin to flow in harmony with something much greater and that is the sacred cycle of life itself.

Part III — Flow, Creativity, and Rebellion as Design

Chapter 7: When Structure Becomes Suppression

There comes a point in every awakening when you realize that the very systems that once kept you safe are now the ones keeping you small. That's what happened to me. For most of my life, I thought structure was salvation. If I could just find the right planner, the right schedule, the right way to organize my day, everything would finally make sense. But structure, for a mind like mine, without freedom, isn't order, it's a cage that looks like safety and I didn't know it yet, but my soul was already pushing against the bars.

The Seduction of Order

There's something comforting about control, about knowing what comes next, about feeling like life can be tamed through lists and routines. Structure makes the world predictable and organized. It keeps chaos at bay but for someone like me, that comfort eventually turns into confinement because I don't thrive in repetition. I thrive in renewal.

I used to force my energy into linear shapes, trying to make it behave. But every time I did, my creativity dimmed. Every time I followed the schedule perfectly, I lost a little more of myself. It took me years to understand why. My mind isn't meant to obey time; it's meant to obey my own rhythm, and rhythm doesn't follow a clock.

The Subtle Prison

The world teaches us that success requires discipline; wake up early, stay organized, stay consistent, plan ahead and for a while, I did all of that. I made charts, color-coded my days, and created rituals to stay productive. On the outside, it worked. But on the inside, something was dying.

Every time I tried to control myself into being "normal," my spirit grew quieter. Every time I forced myself to meet someone else's standard of focus, I lost connection with what made me come alive.

It wasn't laziness that made structure hard for me, it was misalignment because the truth is, not all structure supports you. Some structures are meant to help you grow. Others are meant to keep you small.

The Difference Between Containment and Confinement

I've learned that structure isn't the enemy. It's the intention behind it that matters. **Healthy structure** feels like a riverbank, it gives flow direction without restricting its movement. **Toxic structure** feels like a dam, it blocks the current until the water turns stagnant. For years, I built dams without realizing it. I created systems that looked "responsible" and "put together" but felt lifeless. I mistook rigidity for strength, control for clarity, and exhaustion for success. Until one day, I couldn't sustain it anymore. I was burnt out, uninspired, and numb and that's when I realized that if your structure kills your spirit, it's not discipline, it's suppression.

The Moment I Let Go

It happened quietly. I was sitting at my desk, surrounded by to-do lists and reminders. My planner was full, my day was planned and yet, I felt overwhelmed and empty. Something in me whispered, 'You don't have to live like this' and for the first time, I listened. I closed the planner. I turned off the timer and I asked myself a question I had never asked before: "What does my energy want to do right now?"

At first, it scared me, what if I got nothing done? What if I wasted the day? But what happened next changed everything. I started writing, not out of obligation but out of flow. Hours passed like minutes. The structure dissolved, but my purpose remained. That's when I understood that freedom isn't the absence of structure. It's the presence of alignment.

The Rebellion of Authenticity

There's a quiet rebellion that happens when you stop forcing yourself to fit into the world's rhythm. People will say you've changed. They'll say you've become less reliable, less structured, less predictable but what they won't see is that you've become real because authenticity always looks like rebellion in a world that worships conformity.

I didn't stop caring, I just stopped pretending. I didn't stop working, I started creating differently. I didn't lose focus, I found flow. My life didn't fall apart when I let go of structure. It started to breathe again.

Finding My Own Framework

Eventually, I built new kinds of structures, the kind that honor my nature instead of suppress it. They're soft, fluid, intuitive. They bend with my energy instead of fighting it. Now, I set intentions instead of rules. I follow rhythms instead of routines. I measure success not by how much I do, but by how aligned I feel while doing it. Some days, that means working for hours in full creative focus. Other days, it means resting in silence and letting life rearrange me. Either way, I'm still in motion, it's just a different kind.

Structure as Spiritual Practice

I no longer see structure as a system of control. To me, it's a spiritual tool, a way to give my flow shape without restricting its freedom.

Like breath, inhale and exhale. Structure is the inhale, flow is the exhale. You can't live without either. The key is balance, knowing when to build and when to break, when to hold and when to release.

Every artist knows this and every soul eventually learns it. You can't create without fluidity and container. The secret is knowing which one your spirit needs in the moment.

Freedom as Function

I used to believe structure was what made me functional. Now I know freedom to be who I am is what makes me functional because when I'm free, I'm focused. When I'm aligned, I'm consistent. When I'm honest, I'm efficient. Everything I tried to control through discipline happens naturally when I'm in flow and everything I used to chase through effort unfolds through trust. That's the paradox of ADHD, the less you fight it, the more it works for you. The more you surrender, the stronger you become.

Maybe the world doesn't need more disciplined people. Maybe it needs more aligned ones because discipline without purpose is just control in disguise but alignment, alignment is devotion to truth. In the end, it wasn't structure that saved me. It was the freedom to move with my own rhythm, to flow like I was always meant to because the moment I stopped trying to fit into the world's structure, I became the structure my soul needed all along.

Chapter 8: The Gift They Called Disorder

For years, I believed my existence is a problem. I thought my forgetfulness, my sensitivity, my inability to stay still, all of it meant something was wrong with me. The world told me I had a disorder and I genuinely and seriously believed it because when everyone around you agrees on what's normal, anything that moves differently feels like failure. But what if the world got it wrong? What if what they call disorder is simply a different kind of order, one they haven't learned to see yet?

The Weight of a Label

Labels are powerful things. They shape how we see ourselves, how others treat us, and how we move through life. When I first heard the word ADHD, I didn't even know what it meant. It wasn't part of the vocabulary where I grew up. We didn't talk about neurodivergence, we talked about discipline. So when I was called "lazy" "scatterbrained" , "inattentive," "unmotivated" "anxious" "restless" "unrealiable" I didn't have language to defend myself. I just carried those words like quiet wounds. That's what labels do when they come from misunderstanding, they don't explain you; they confine you. But eventually, something shifted. The more I learned about ADHD, the more I realized, this wasn't a disease. It was just a different way of being.

Attention: Deep And Not Deficient

The world defines ADHD by what it lacks "Deficit." But if you've lived inside this mind, you know that's not true. We don't lack attention; we have too much of it. Our attention is like sunlight, vast, energized, radiant, and vibrant. It doesn't disappear; it just moves toward what matters most. That's why we can't force focus on things that don't align within us. That's why we lose ourselves in what we love. We don't have attention deficit, we have attention depth. It's just that the system doesn't know how to measure that kind of brilliance.

Hyperactivity: Energy in Translation

Then there's the "H" — Hyperactivity. They say it like it's a flaw. But what if it's just life force that refuses to shrink? We don't sit still because we're not supposed to. We're meant to move energy. Our restlessness is direction. It's the body's way of releasing excess energy that the world keeps trying to suppress. The problem isn't the movement. It's how it is misunderstood.

Our energy is a communication. It's how spirit flows through our body, how inspiration becomes action and once you stop fighting it, that same restlessness becomes our creativity in motion.

Disorder: Or Divine Design?

And then there's that word — **Disorder.** The heaviest of them all.

It implies something is wrong, broken, in need of correction. But I've learned that disorder is only seen as such when you measure it through the lens of uniformity. Nature itself is full of what humans would call "disorder." Waves crash unevenly. Branches twist in every direction. Lightning never strikes the same way twice. Yet everything in nature, even its chaotic follows divine pattern. So what makes us any different? Maybe our minds aren't disordered. Maybe they're designed differently. Maybe what the system calls "abnormal" is just a frequency it doesn't understand yet.

A Different Kind of Intelligence

I used to envy people who could think linearly, who could stay calm, organized, methodical. But now I see that my mind works in constellations and not lines. I don't think step by step; I think in patterns. I see the whole picture at once; the emotional, the symbolic, the energetic, the practical, all connected in one instant. It's not that I can't think logically. It's that I think organically.

My thoughts move like nature, unpredictable yet intelligent. They bloom, retreat, return, evolve. That's why I can see solutions others overlook, sense connections that don't exist on paper, and bring creativity into chaos because my mind was never meant to fit inside boxes, it was meant to create new shapes.

The Hidden Superpower

Here's what they don't tell you about ADHD: We are visionaries by design. We feel faster, sense deeper, and process more. We move at the speed of inspiration. Our minds are open. We see what others miss because we notice everything. We feel what others suppress because our empathy is awake. We imagine what others fear because we've lived in the in-between. That's why the world has always struggled to understand us because we are here to expand it.

We were never meant to blend in; we were meant to bring color to the ordinary. What others call impulsive is often our courage to act before fear takes over. What others call formless is the birth of creation. Our minds move like constellations, connecting stars no one else sees. We don't just think outside the box; we dissolve the box completely. The world may not always understand how we move, but every revolution begins with those who were once misunderstood.

The System Was Built for Predictability

The real problem isn't the ADHD mind, it's the system that only rewards one kind of intelligence. Schools, workplaces, institutions, they're designed for predictability. They measure success by output. So when someone comes along who moves differently, they call it a defect. But difference is the birthplace of every evolution humanity has ever known. The thinkers, inventors, artists, visionaries; all of them were once labeled difficult, distracted, or defiant. So maybe we were never supposed to fit in. Maybe we were designed to break the pattern, to show the world that there are other ways to live, learn, and lead.

I know what it feels like to sit in a room that was never built for you. To be told to focus harder when your mind is already working overtime just to stay present. To be measured by standards that never recognized how you think, feel, or create. That's the quiet pain of sameness, it erases individuality in the name of order. But being the same was never the point of being human. We were meant to bring different colors, different rhythms, different ways of seeing into the collective. And maybe that's why we were born with minds that don't fit, to remind the world that brilliance doesn't always look like discipline. Sometimes, it looks like difference.

The Reframe That Changed Everything

The moment I stopped asking, "What's wrong with me?" and started asking, "What's right about me that the world doesn't see?" everything changed. I realized my sensitivity wasn't a flaw, it was intuition. My restlessness wasn't distraction, it was divine movement. My impulsiveness wasn't recklessness, it was courage in raw form. My curiosity was genius in motion. Once I saw it that way, the shame lifted because I finally realized that I was simply misunderstood.

That moment of reframing didn't just change how I saw myself, it changed how I experienced life. I began to move with my own rhythm, to listen to the quiet intelligence beneath the noise. Every trait I once judged became a teacher. My energy, my emotions, my curiosity, they were never flaws to fix; they were whispers from my soul reminding me of who I am and maybe that's the real healing, not becoming someone new, but finally remembering that nothing about you was ever wrong. You were just waiting to see yourself through gentler eyes.

The Gift Hidden in the Name

ADHD — four letters that once made me feel defective.

Now, they feel like a code I've learned to translate differently:

Awareness

Driven by

Higher

Design

It's not a medical term anymore, it's a spiritual one. It means I process life through sensitivity, movement, and multidimensional awareness. It means my focus isn't missing; it's sacredly selective. It means my brain doesn't obey logic because it's wired for intuition. And that's not a curse. That's capacity of owning the brilliance. Once I understood this, I stopped trying to heal myself from being who I am. Healing isn't about changing your wiring, it's about understanding it.

My brilliance may not look like order, but it works in perfect design. It's the kind of intelligence that feels the world before it defines it. That creates before it explains. That understands before it categorizes. And maybe that's why we're here, not to be normal, but to remind the world what real intelligence feels like.

What they diagnose as dysfunction, I experience as divinity, the mind of a creator trying to live in a world built for repetition. My attention isn't scattered. My energy isn't wrong. My difference isn't a flaw. It's all evidence of the gift. And maybe, in time, the world will stop calling it ADHD and start calling it what it truly is:

A Different Harmony of Divine.

Chapter 9: The World That Can't Keep Up

Sometimes I think the world moves too fast for itself. Everything is instant communication, entertainment, validation. We're more connected than ever, yet somehow more divided inside and in that noise, the ADHD mind, the one that moves by intuition, emotion, and rhythm feels both ahead of its time and left behind by it because the truth is, the world doesn't know how to move with people like us. It only knows how to manage us.

But here's the irony: The same world that calls us "too much," "too scattered," or "too sensitive" is now becoming more like us. Constant stimulation. Multiple tabs open. Notifications firing off every second. Everyone's attention divided, everyone's energy scattered. The world has become ADHD and it's struggling to keep up with itself.

The Age of Overstimulation

We live in an attention economy. Everything from the apps on your phone to the ads in your feed is designed to capture your focus and hold it hostage. The average person now experiences more stimuli in one day than entire generations did in a lifetime. No wonder our nervous systems are overwhelmed but for those of us who've always lived this way; constantly scanning, absorbing, connecting, this chaos feels oddly familiar. It's as if the rest of the world has stepped into our operating system, and now everyone's realizing how intense it can be. Except for us, it's not new. It's home.

Born for a Faster Frequency

ADHD minds are built for speed, it's not in a mechanical way, but in an energetic one. We move through ideas faster, feel frequencies faster, process emotion faster. That's why the modern world feels both overstimulating and undernourishing. It gives us too much to process, but too little that matters. We can scroll for hours and not feel fed. We can have constant communication and still feel unseen.

We crave depth in a world addicted to distraction. We were built for meaning, not noise and the world, as it is right now, is choking on its own stimulation. We sense it before others do because our nervous systems are mirrors. We feel the world's imbalance inside our own bodies.

The Myth of Productivity

Modern society measures worth by output. How much did you get done? How fast did you finish? How consistent can you stay? But for those of us who live through rhythm and resonance, productivity means something different. It's not about how much we do, it's about how much align we pour into what we do. We don't move by the clock; we move by connection. That's why burnout feels spiritual for us, it's not just fatigue; it's a sign that we've been working against our nature.

In a system that glorifies endless doing, being still feels like rebellion. But for ADHD souls, rest isn't laziness, it's our recalibration. We're not lazy, we're listening because we're waiting for alignment and when it arrives, we move with force and brilliance.

Technology Imitating the ADHD Mind

If you think about it, technology itself has begun to mirror the ADHD brain. Infinite tabs. Multitasking. Constant dopamine loops. Everything demanding attention, all at once. The internet doesn't move in lines; it moves in connections just like we do. The difference is that we can feel what's meaningful through it, while technology can't. It replicates our rhythm but not our soul. That's what makes us human, our ability to feel through the noise and sense what's real beneath the static. Maybe the ADHD mind isn't lagging behind evolution. Maybe it is evolution, showing us what consciousness looks like when it's moving faster than structure.

Maybe that's why we were born into this era, to remind the world that connection without consciousness isn't progress. The ADHD mind was never meant to compete with technology; it was meant to humanize it. To bring heart back into speed, intuition back into information, and meaning back into motion. In a world that's constantly updating, our presence is the real upgrade because when awareness meets acceleration, evolution finally becomes alive.

When the World Rewards Numbness

Sometimes I look around and wonder if the system actually rewards disconnection. People who don't feel too much. People who can shut off empathy to survive. People who can follow without questioning.

It's almost as if sensitivity has become rebellion because to feel deeply in a world that numbs itself is to disrupt the pattern. But ADHD doesn't allow numbness. We feel everything, sometimes all at once.

We pick up on emotional frequencies that others overlook in conversations, spaces, even silences. That sensitivity is our gift. It's how we read the undercurrents of life and if the world is going to evolve, it will need that kind of awareness not less of it.

So I stopped apologizing for feeling deeply. I stopped shrinking my sensitivity just to make others comfortable because the truth is, I'd rather feel everything than feel nothing at all. I'd rather live awake than sleepwalk through a world that calls emptiness strength. My emotions don't make me fragile, they make me feel alive and in a world that rewards numbness, staying open is the most radical thing I can do.

The Future Belongs to the Fluid

The systems built on rigidity are collapsing; education, work, politics, economics. They were designed for predictability, not adaptability.

But the future requires flexibility, minds that can think in patterns, pivot quickly, and sense where energy is moving before logic can catch up. That's what we do naturally. We don't follow trends; we feel them before they form. We don't cling to plans; we move with purpose as it unfolds. We're not scattered, we're just spherical.

Our awareness expands in every direction, touching multiple realities at once. That's why linear systems can't keep up with us, they weren't built to move multidimensionally but the future will be. The next era of humanity will belong to the ones who can flow and not just think. To those who can sense energy and not just analyze data. To those who can imagine new systems that feel human again and that's what the ADHD mind was built for.

The Mirror and the Medicine

What if we're not the problem, but the reflection? What if our so-called "symptoms" are actually signals, mirrors showing the collective where it's out of balance? Our restlessness points to stagnation. Our distraction reveals over-saturation. Our impulsivity exposes the lack of spontaneity in a controlled world. We are both the mirror and the medicine. The world judges what it doesn't understand but every misunderstood gift is also a map. We show the way back to intuition, creativity, and emotional honesty because we live in a world that's forgotten how to feel, and our very existence reminds it to remember.

Maybe that's the higher purpose of our difference, to heal the collective by reflecting it. We don't have to save the world; we just have to stay true to what we feel, and in doing so, we become the frequency of truth itself. Our sensitivity isn't a flaw in the design, it is the design. Every emotion we carry, every thought that won't quiet, every spark that refuses to die is part of the medicine because when we stop trying to hide what we are, the world begins to remember what it's been missing.

When the World Finally Slows Down

Sometimes I imagine a world that finally moves at the right pace, not through rushed or rigid, just real. A world where schools teach emotional intelligence before memorization. Where work honors rest as part of creation. Where children are guided and not corrected, for how their minds move. That's the world I want to help build not by fighting the system, because the system is our foundation, but by living proof that another way is possible because the moment I stopped trying to catch up with the world, I realized it was the world that needed to catch up with me.

Maybe we were never meant to keep up. Maybe we were meant to remind the world to slow down. To move with meaning, create with feeling and live with depth instead of speed because what they call distraction, impulsive, or disorder, I call it genetic design. The world can't keep up with us, it's not because we're ahead or behind but because we've already evolved into what it's still becoming.

Part IV —
Gratitude for the Gift

Chapter 10: Brilliance in Motion

There was a time when I thought my brilliance needed to be earned. That I had to prove it, perfect it, polish it before I could call it mine. But now I know brilliance doesn't come from effort. It comes from essence. It's what shines through when you stop trying to be anything other than what you are. My brilliance was never in how still I could sit, how neatly I could think, or how consistent I could perform. It was always in how freely I could move, how truth flowed through me when I stopped resisting myself because the gift of ADHD isn't in what we control but in how we allow it.

Maybe the real brilliance was never in doing more, but in being true. In letting ourselves exist without the weight of proving. When we finally stop fighting who we are, something gentle happens, life starts flowing through us instead of against us. That's when our light feels effortless, something we become.

The Beauty of Uncontainable Energy

There's something miraculous about a mind that can't be contained. For so long, I resented it the way it jumped from one idea to another, the way it refused to slow down, the way it burned with a thousand directions at once but now, I see the beauty in that space of existence. It's the same energy that creates galaxies. The same movement that makes stars collide and flowers bloom. To have that energy inside you that is untamed and unstoppable is a gift, even when it doesn't feel like one. Life itself is motion and we, the ones who can't sit still, are simply mirrors of that motion. We are the embodiment of energy that refuses to go numb. We are proof that creation never sleeps.

Creation was never meant to be orderly. Maybe chaos was the first language of the universe, a wild pulse that knew exactly what it was becoming even before form existed. Stars didn't ask for permission to burn; they just did. Oceans didn't wait to be contained; they overflowed into being. That same divine unrest lives in us. We are fragments of that first explosion, carrying the memory of motion itself. Our minds, our sparks, our endless ideas, they are proof that creation is still happening, through us, as us.

Living as a Channel, Not a Controller

Somewhere along my journey, I stopped trying to control my energy and started to channel it. Instead of asking, "How can I fix this?" I began to ask, "How can I use this?" That small shift changed everything. Now, when inspiration floods me, I follow it. When emotion rises, I listen to it. When energy moves, I move with it.

I stopped demanding stillness from myself. I started respecting my current, the way it moves, changes, and flows with divine timing because maybe that's what brilliance really is, the willingness to be a vessel for something larger than logic. I don't think my way through life anymore; I feel my way through it and somehow, it always leads me exactly where I need to go.

The Power of Sensitivity

My sensitivity used to feel like a burden. Every sound, every emotion, every subtle shift in the air, I felt it all. But sensitivity, when you understand it, is sacred intelligence. It's the soul's way of gathering information that the mind can't see. I sense when something is off before it's spoken. I feel creative direction before words appear. I know when a room is heavy and when it's healing. It's not a flaw. That's intuition in its purest form and I call it connection because feeling everything is how I stay close to life itself.

Sensitivity is how the divine speaks through us quietly, softly, through goosebumps, tears, and the rhythm of our hearts. It's something to honor. The world teaches us to toughen up, to filter out, to numb what's too much but the truth is, sensitivity is strength in its most graceful form. It's what allows us to touch the invisible, to love without reason, to hear what the world has forgotten to say. When we stop apologizing for feeling so deeply, we realize we were simply tuned to a higher kind of listening.

The Dance Between Focus and Flow

There's a dance between my mind and my energy that I've learned to trust; a rhythm that only makes sense when I stop trying to control it. Some days, I am all fire; ideas, movement, creation. Other days, I am water; slow, still, reflective and both are divine. Both are part of the brilliance.

When I'm in flow, my mind becomes a universe. When I'm in stillness, my soul becomes a mirror. Neither one is better. They just need each other because the truth is, brilliance isn't a spark that burns once, it's a flame that learns to breathe.

That's why I no longer fight the shifts in my energy. I let them teach me. Some days I burn bright, some days I fade into quiet, and both are holy in their own way. I've learned that focus means presence and flow is trust. Somewhere between the two, I found peace with who I am and how I move.

The Joy of Reframing

What once made me ashamed now makes me smile. Forgetting things? My brain was clearing space for new ideas. Talking too much? I was trying to translate the energy moving through me. Restless at night? My spirit wasn't done processing the day. Everything I used to judge has a reason. Everything I used to fight has wisdom. My ADHD doesn't need to be cured, it needs to be celebrated because what looks like disorder on the outside often holds divine harmony on the inside and once you see it, you can't unsee it.

Maybe that's what returning to self really is, learning to love what once confused you. To see beauty where you used to see flaw. My mind was never working against me; it was teaching me to move differently, to listen deeper, to trust the divine rhythm that flows through me. Now, I don't chase normal, I honor natural. Every quirk, every spark, every shift is a quiet reminder that who I am genetically was never a mistake.

Learning to Receive Ease

The hardest thing for me was learning how to receive ease. To stop earning my right to rest. To stop turning my brilliance into proof. For so long, I thought I had to hustle to deserve peace but peace doesn't come from effort; it comes from acceptance. Now, I let life move through me without forcing the rhythm. If inspiration comes, I flow. If silence comes, I honor it. My life stopped feeling like a chase the moment I stopped trying to control it. That's when I finally understood; freedom doesn't come from doing more. It comes from being more of yourself.

Ease, I've learned, is the presence of trust. It's the quiet knowing that I don't have to chase what's already aligned with me. The moment I stopped gripping, life started giving. Now, every breath feels like an offering and every pause a prayer. I no longer measure my worth by movement. I measure it by how gently I can let life love me back.

Brilliance as Service

The more I accept my design, the more I realize, my brilliance isn't for me alone, it's for others too. Every idea I share, every connection I make, every insight I express, it ripples outward because energy never stops with you. It moves through you. ADHD has made me a vessel for movement of thought, creativity, and emotion. It's taught me that service isn't always planned; sometimes it's spontaneous, impulsive, intuitive, perfectly unorganized and yet, profoundly impactful. My purpose was never to be perfect. It was to move truth through me and that's what my brilliance does, it reminds others that it's safe to move, to feel, to be different, to live in motion.

Because brilliance, when shared, becomes light. It doesn't belong to the one who carries it, it belongs to everyone it touches. The more I let it flow through me without control, the more it finds its way to those who need it. Service is something I become when I stop trying to contain what's meant to move.

Gratitude for the Wild Design

If I could go back and talk to my younger self, the one sitting in class, confused, restless and ashamed. I'd tell her that she was never behind. She was just tuned to a different frequency. The world couldn't understand her rhythm because it hadn't learned to dance yet. But one day, she will. She'll see that her pace was perfect, her pattern was divine, and her way of seeing the world was never a mistake. It was brilliance in motion because that is what I am seeing now.

Brilliance isn't a trait. It's a state, one that appears when you finally stop resisting your nature. You don't have to try to shine. You just have to stop dimming what's already there. ADHD isn't my limitation. It's my language, the way my soul speaks through energy, emotion, and intuition. I am no longer ashamed of the way I move because movement is my medicine. It's how I connect, create and live. My mind doesn't sit still because it was never meant to. It was meant to move the world.

Chapter 11: For Every Mind That Ever Felt Wrong

This is for the ones who always felt a step behind in a world that never slowed down. For the ones who grew up being told they were too much, too messy, too sensitive and too distracted. For the ones who tried to fit in and found themselves fading instead. This is for the child who stared out the classroom window and got scolded for dreaming. For the teenager who couldn't follow the rules but followed their heart instead. For the adult who still apologizes for not being like everyone else. This is for every mind that ever felt wrong.

You Were Never Broken

You were never the problem. The system just wasn't built for your rhythm. It was designed for uniformity, for straight lines and quiet obedience while you were made of curves and sound and light. You were born to feel, not to conform. You were wired to wonder, not to memorize. You were designed to move, not to sit still in someone else's idea of success. The world measured your value by how well you could follow its rules, but your soul never agreed to that contract because you were never meant to be a copy. You were born as a reminder of what originality feels like.

You Move Differently Because You're Alive Differently

Your energy doesn't move in straight lines, it spirals, expands, circles back, transforms. That's not dysfunction. That's evolution. You're not unfocused, you're deeply attuned. You're not inconsistent, you're cyclical. You're not scattered, you're spherical, touching multiple dimensions of life at once.

You were designed to sense what others overlook, the emotion behind the word, the truth beneath the surface, the pulse inside the silence. You are not here to fit the pattern. You are here to feel it shift.

What They Called Defect Was Design

They called it distraction when your attention followed beauty, impulsive when your instincts spoke faster than logic, hyper when your body overflowed with aliveness, disorder when you refused to numb yourself to fit the world's convenience but what they couldn't see was this is that you were never trying to escape reality; you were trying to make it real. You were born with a sensitivity that doesn't just observe life, it absorbs it. That's not a flaw. That's frequency. You feel what others miss because you're tuned to the subtleties that most have forgotten to notice and that's brilliance.

The Art of Remembering Who You Are

The healing doesn't happen the moment you get a diagnosis or read a definition. It happens when you start to remember yourself. When you stop chasing who you think you should be, and return to the one who already knows who she is. When you forgive yourself for the years spent trying to earn peace. When you realize there was never anything to fix only something to understand. Expansion isn't about turning off your energy; it's about learning its language. It's about letting your rhythm lead again. It's about trusting that your difference was never the detour, it was always the path.

You Are the New Definition

The world will continue to evolve, but its voices like yours that shape how it does. Every time you choose authenticity over approval, you rewrite the meaning of intelligence. Every time you embrace your sensitivity instead of apologizing for it, you teach the world what empathy looks like in motion. Every time you follow your flow instead of forcing focus, you give others permission to trust their truth. You are the new definition of awareness, living proof that brilliance doesn't have to look like control. You are not behind. You are beyond.

The Quiet Bravery of Being Yourself

It takes courage to live in a world that misunderstands your genetics. It takes even more to love yourself that doesn't ask for permission, that doesn't need proof. It's what changes everything because the moment you stop running from your difference, you start radiating what you were always meant to give.

You start living in a way that feels like breathing, creating in a way that feels like remembering and existing in a way that no longer hurts. It's homecoming.

A Letter to the Reader

If you've made it this far, Thank you. Thank you for reading, for listening, and for letting me share the language of my mind, the way my thoughts, emotions, and spirit dance together in their own rhythm.

And if you've ever doubted your worth because you couldn't follow the rules, remember this that the rules were never written for you. You came here to write new ones. Your mind, the one that moves fast and feels deeply, was never a problem to fix. It is the universe remembering how to create through human form. You are exactly enough. You are not scattered; you are infinite and you are not behind; you are multidimensional and when the world finally catches up, it will look at people like you and whisper, 'they were the map all along.'

A map to learn how to honor the structure without losing your flow. We began to see that discipline is not control, it's grounding. Boundaries are not cages, they are roots. Every energy needs something to hold it, and Earth, in her wisdom, gives us that. She is the foundation and the form that allows our movement to have meaning. Think of her as the stage upon which our art unfolds. Our ADHD being; our colors, our rhythms, our chaos, our spark needs that stage to be seen. Without it, our brilliance would remain invisible potential. The Earth gives it visibility. She provides the contrast so that our light can be witnessed, so that what moves within us can finally find a form others can recognize.

We, the ones who move differently, are not here to destroy order. We are here to expand it, to remind the world that movement and density can exist together, that disorder can become creation when it finds a home inside form. Maybe the point was never to overcome ADHD. Maybe it was to understand that brilliance and chaos were never enemies, they were partners in creation all along. Maybe this journey was never about fixing your attention but about falling in love with how it dances. The truth is, our rhythm isn't wrong. It's just different. It's alive and real. It's the pulse of evolution moving through us.

So, if you ever feel misunderstood, if you ever wonder why you don't move like everyone else, remember that you were never meant to. You were born to teach the world a new way of moving, a new way of thinking, a new way of being human. Your sensitivity is wisdom. Your energy is creation. Your attention is divine curiosity reaching for what truly matters.

Honor the laws of the Earth, but don't lose the song of your soul. Respect the structure, but keep your flow in motion. Let your difference lead you back to the truth, that every system needs a little bit of disruption to remember how to breathe. You are that breath. You are that reminder. You are that movement. You are brilliance in motion. You always have been. And now, you finally remember it.

Warm Hugs and Kisses,
— Sheila Mae Balaga

Acknowledgement

To every teacher who couldn't quite understand me, **Thank you.**
You taught me how to see beyond instruction, how to listen to my own rhythm when the world demanded perfection.

To the systems that called me "Rebellious" **Thank you** for showing me what it means to create my own way of being, for every boundary you placed became a doorway into my own freedom.

To my family; for your patience, love, and quiet faith. **Thank you.** You held me in seasons when I couldn't hold myself. You let me take the long way home to my truth, and in that space, I found grace.

To my friends who never tried to fix me, **Thank you** for seeing the beauty in my difference. For laughing with me when my thoughts leaped between galaxies, or as you called it in my "la la land moments" and for reminding me that presence doesn't always need structure, sometimes, it just needs understanding, unconditional love and acceptance.

To the ones who read these words and whisper, that's me, Thank you.
You are the reason I wrote this. Every misunderstood child, every restless adult, every creative heart who felt wrong for being wired differently. You are the quiet revolution I believe in. You are the art this world forgot it needed.

To this Earth, the foundation that holds my motion, the stage where my mind can perform its sacred dance. Thank you for being patient with our evolution, for giving us gravity when our thoughts fly too far, and for letting our wildness have somewhere to land.

To the unseen forces, the whispers, the intuition, the divine timing that guided every word, **Thank you.** You wrote this book through me. Every sentence was a conversation between my soul and something greater.

And finally, **to my own mind,** for its fire, its rhythm, its sensitivity and its endless curiosity. For all the times I wished you were different, and for the day I finally realized you were my greatest gift.

Thank you for bringing me home to myself.

Stay Connected with Me

Thank you for taking the time to read I Have ADHD, Why Not?
I hope this book reminded you that your brilliance was never meant to fit inside anyone else's definition of structure.

If you'd like to continue exploring your energy, your emotions, and your rhythm, you can connect with me through my work and creations below:

Tap to Shift App
An emotional reset app designed to help you pause, reflect, and realign using my 8A Method.

Available on:
App Store
Google Play

Learn more:
www.taptoshift.com

Website & Socials
Website: www.taptoshift.ccm
Instagram: @ihaveadhdwhynot
LinkedIn: www.linkedin.com/in/sheilamaebalaga

Thank you for being here — for reading, feeling, and shifting with me.

With so much love,
Sheila Mae Balaga